I0816211

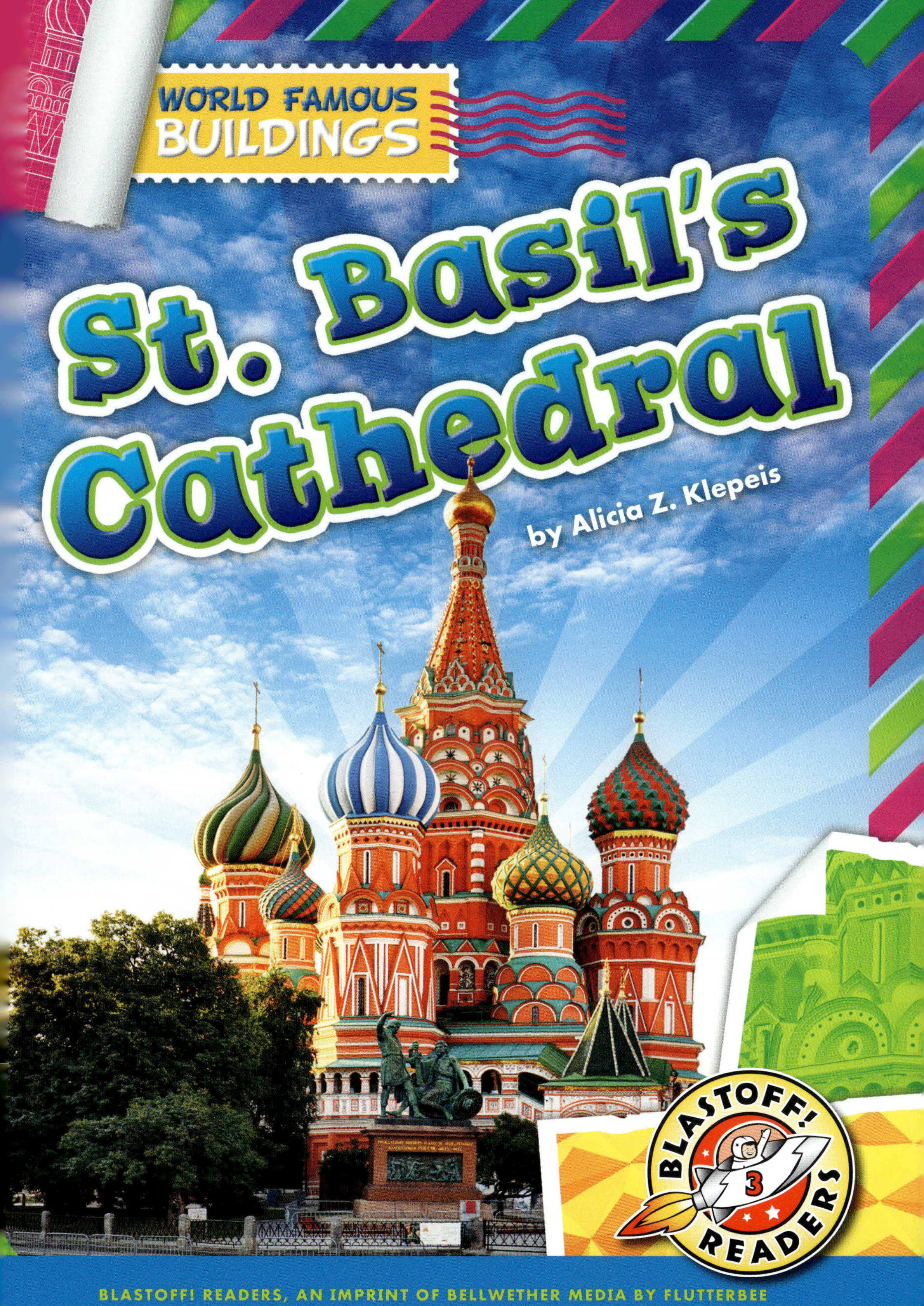

BLASTOFF! READERS, AN IMPRINT OF BELLWETHER MEDIA BY FLUTTERBEE

Blastoff! Readers are carefully developed by literacy experts to build reading stamina and move students toward fluency by combining standards-based content with developmentally appropriate text.

LEVELS

Level 1 provides the most support through repetition of high-frequency words, light text, predictable sentence patterns, and strong visual support.

Level 2 offers early readers a bit more challenge through varied sentences, increased text load, and text-supportive special features.

Level 3 advances early-fluent readers toward fluency through increased text load, less reliance on photos, advancing concepts, longer sentences, and more complex special features.

★ **Blastoff! Universe**

Reading Level

Grade K

Grades 1–3

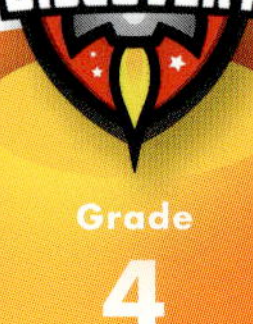

Grade 4

This edition first published in 2026 by Bellwether Media, Inc.

For information regarding permission, write to Bellwether Media, Inc., Attention: Permissions Department, 3500 American Blvd W, Suite 150, Bloomington, MN 55431.

Library of Congress Cataloging-in-Publication Data is available at www.loc.gov or upon request from the publisher.

ISBN: 9798893048094 (hardcover)
ISBN: 9798893049091 (ebook)

Editor: Betsy Rathburn Designer: Laura Sowers

Printed in the United States of America, North Mankato, MN.

Table of Contents

What Is St. Basil's Cathedral?

St. Basil's **Cathedral** is an **Orthodox** church in Moscow, Russia. It towers above Red Square. This is the site of many important events in Russian history.

The building is famous for its colorful **onion domes**.

St. Basil's Cathedral is a museum. Visitors come from around the world to see its artwork. They learn about its **architecture**.

Some people go to **religious** services here.

History of St. Basil's Cathedral

Tsar Ivan IV was Russia's ruler in the mid-1500s. He ordered a cathedral to be built. It would celebrate his military success.

Building began in 1555.

Ivan IV

1800s art of St. Basil's Cathedral

Workers used white stone for the **foundation**. They built the building's frame from wood.

Brick was uncommon in Russia at the time. Builders used it to cover the frame. Construction lasted six years.

Parts of St. Basil's Cathedral

The cathedral has a large **chapel** at its center. Eight smaller chapels surround it.

Another chapel was added in 1588. It honors Saint Basil. A bell tower was added later.

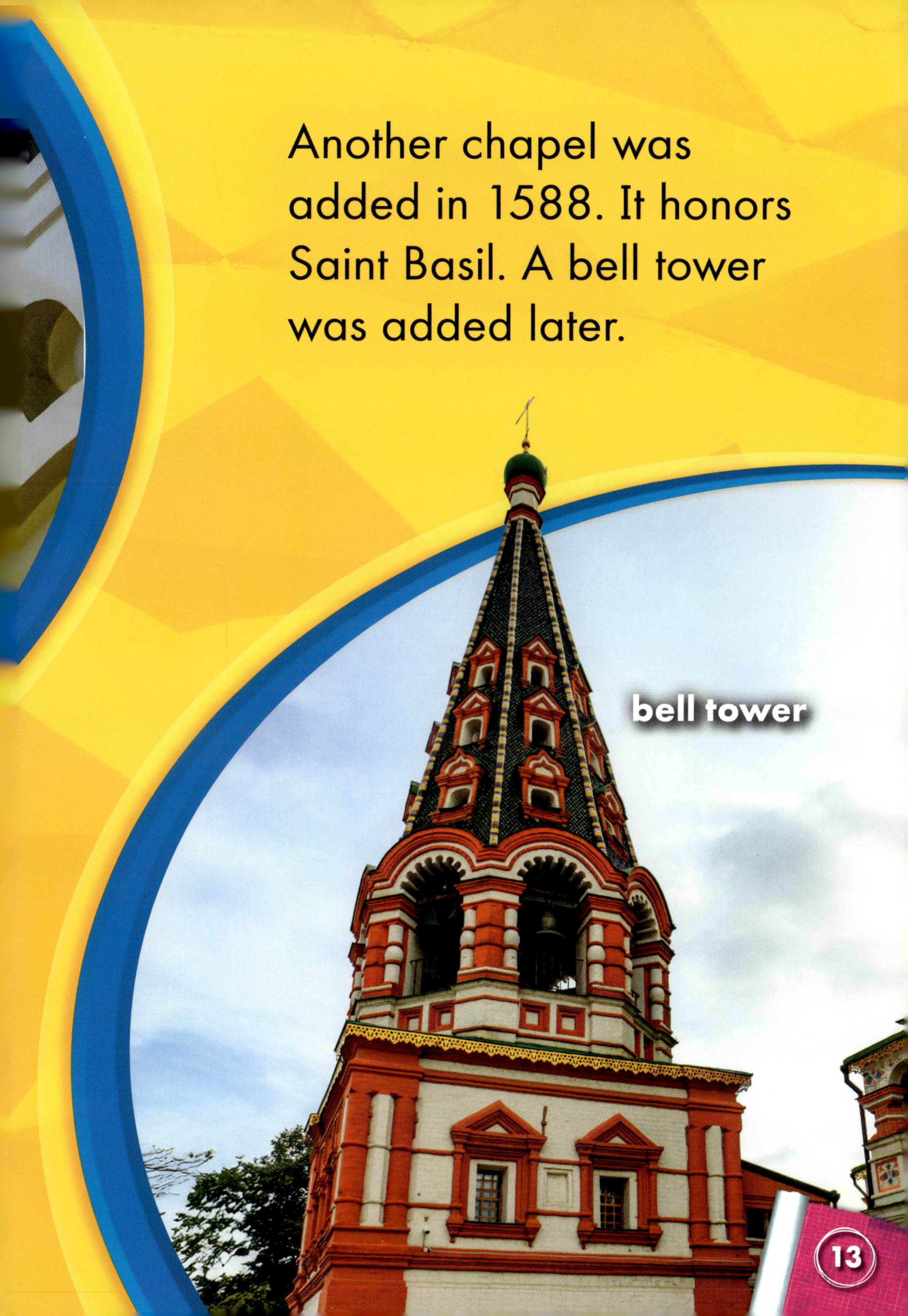

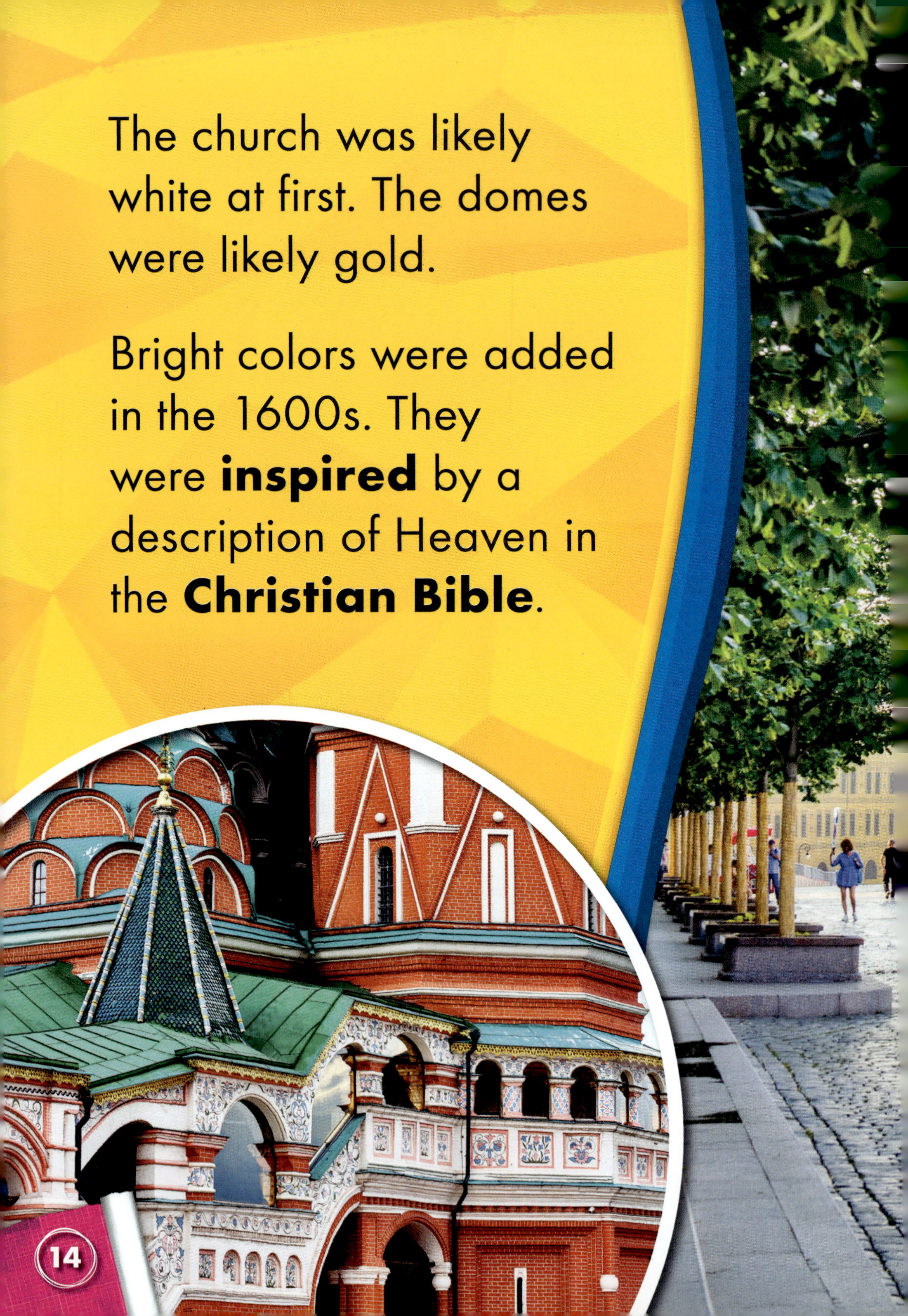

The church was likely white at first. The domes were likely gold.

Bright colors were added in the 1600s. They were **inspired** by a description of Heaven in the **Christian Bible**.

Onion Domes

Number of Domes nine

Made From wood, metal

Art fills the inside of the building. Many paintings show religious figures. Others are of plants or pretty patterns.

Wooden carvings and fancy lights add to the cathedral's beauty.

St. Basil's Cathedral Today

Fires have damaged
St. Basil's during its history.
War has too.

A major **restoration** project took place in the early 2000s. Crews repainted its domes. They repaired many paintings.

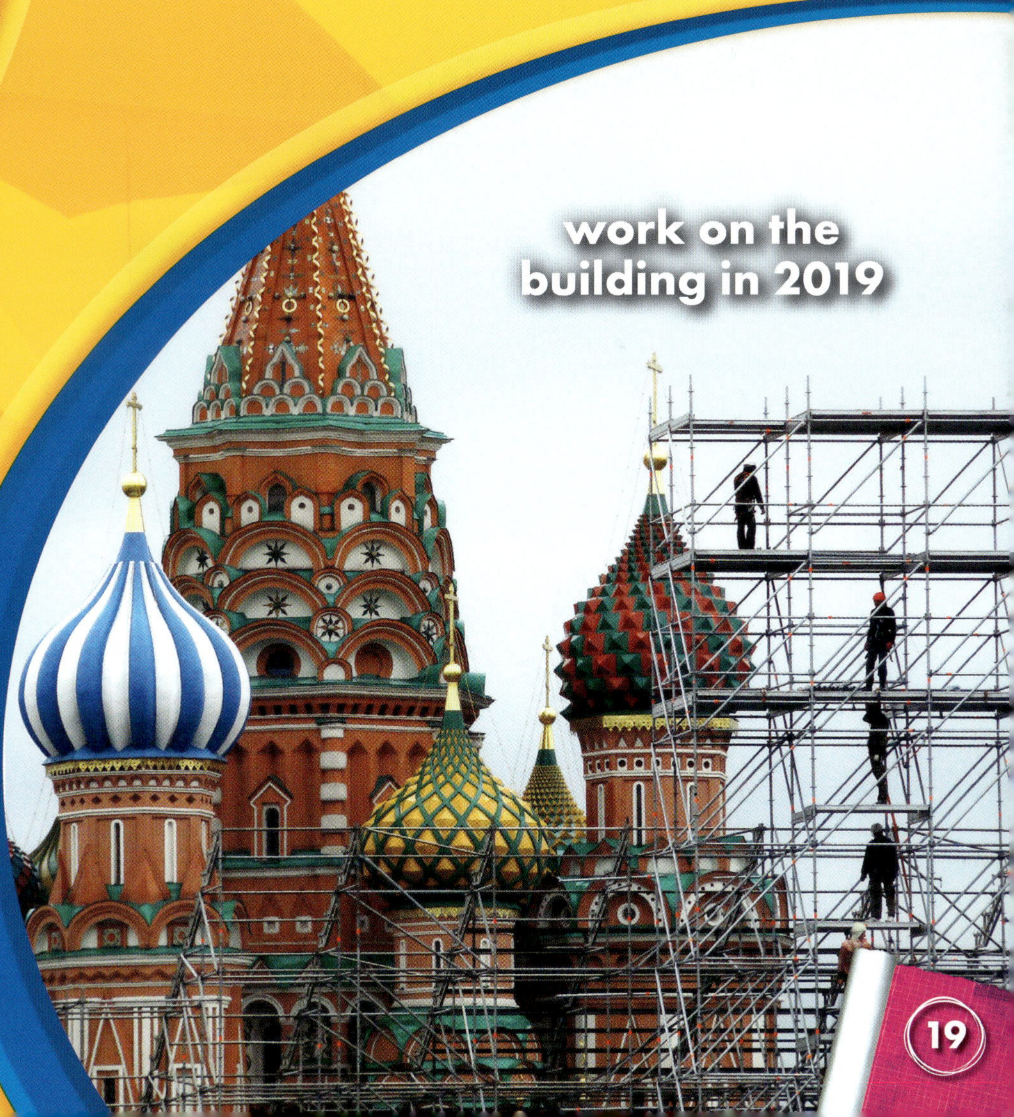

work on the building in 2019

Hundreds of thousands of **tourists** visit the cathedral each year. It is one of Russia's most popular places to visit.

Its colorful domes are sure to attract visitors far into the future!

tourists

Glossary

architecture—the design and structure of buildings

cathedral—an important church

chapel—a small church

Christian Bible—the holy book of Christianity; the Christian Bible includes the Old Testament and the New Testament.

foundation—the base or support on which a building rests

inspired—given an idea about what to do or create

onion domes—rounded roofs on buildings that are wide in the middle and come to a point at the top

Orthodox—a type of Christianity common in Eastern Europe, especially Greece and Russia

religious—having to do with a certain faith

restoration—the process of repairing a building

tourists—people who travel to visit another place

tsar—a ruler of Russia

To Learn More

AT THE LIBRARY

Klepeis, Alicia Z. *Sagrada Familia.* Minneapolis, Minn.: Bellwether Media, 2026.

Reynolds, Donna, and Kaitlyn Duling. *Russia.* Buffalo, N.Y.: Cavendish Square Publishing, 2025.

Sabelko, Rebecca. *Russia.* Minneapolis, Minn.: Bellwether Media, 2023.

ON THE WEB

FACTSURFER

Factsurfer.com gives you a safe, fun way to find more information.

1. Go to www.factsurfer.com.
2. Enter "St. Basil's Cathedral" into the search box and click 🔍.
3. Select your book cover to see a list of related content.

Index

The images in this book are reproduced through the courtesy of: TTstudio, front cover; dimbar76, front cover (inset 1); Vladitto, front cover (inset 2); f11photo, p. 3; yulenochekk, pp. 4-5, 18-19; Lagutkin Alexey, pp. 6-7; volkova Natalia, pp. 8-9; anonym/ Wikipedia, p. 9 (Ivan IV); Ipsumpix/ Getty Images, p. 9; AleksandarGeorgiev, p. 10; Kateryna Muzhevska, p. 11 (white stone); romantiche, p. 11 (wood); arybickii, p. 11 (brick); Yury Gubin, p. 11; Pommy.Anyani, pp. 12-13, 16-17; Olha Solodenko, p. 13; Fnadya76, p. 14; E. O., pp. 14-15; SimoneGilioli, p. 15; dimdiz, p. 19; Kay Roxby/ Alamy Stock Photo, p. 20; Andrey Danilovich, pp. 20-21; Parilov, p. 23.